KINGDOM MANDATE

A WAKE UP CALL FOR THE CHURCH

"But this Man, after He had offered one sacrifice for sins forever, sat down at the right hand of God, from that time waiting till His enemies are made His footstool" (Hebrews 10:12-13).

ABRAHAM JOHN

Kingdom Mandate: A Wake up Call for the Church
Copyright © 2016 by Abraham John
Published by Abraham John

Maximum Impact Ministries
P.O. Box 631460
Littleton, CO 80163-1460

www.maximpact.org
email: mim@maximpact.org
(720) 420 9873

ISBN: 978-0-9972591-0-0

Printed and published in the U.S.A

Contents

The *Next* Move of God

Preface

For too long the body of Christ has been waiting for the revival or rapture, but let me tell you the good news: The greatest move of God we have all been waiting for is right here in the midst of us. In fact, it started almost two thousand years ago! It is called the kingdom movement. Though this movement has been among us for many years, the church as a whole has yet to catch up with it. The time has come for us to fully cooperate with God in what He wants to do here on earth.

Why the kingdom movement? Throughout the centuries the church has been asking God for particular benefits and specializing in a few aspects of the kingdom. As a result He sent the healing movement, salvation movement, holiness movement, word of faith movement, and others. They are all different aspects of His kingdom, but not *the* kingdom. The time has come for us to receive the whole kingdom and administer it so that God's will is done on the earth *as it is in heaven.*

Why, in nations where Christians are the majority, do they have no influence in decision-making? Why are nations where mighty revivals once took place now considered post-Christian societies? Why do some nations where Christians are the majority remain poor? Why do the majority of people on this earth remain unreached when two thousand years ago just twelve men reached almost the whole known world in their own lifetime? This is what happens when the church fails to administer the kingdom of God.

I believe there is still hope for the church in the West, but we need to take some emergency steps if we are to turn the ship before it gets wrecked. Just because the church is God's idea does not mean harm won't come to it. History proves that bad things can happen to churches and nations if they don't heed the voice of God, even if they are chosen by Him. We are all familiar with the history of Israel.

The seven churches named in the book of Revelation don't exist today. All of the great churches that Paul established disappeared from the face of the earth. Europe—once known as the cradle of Christianity and world missions—is now considered a post-Christian society. Many hide behind a form of religion because they know it is written in the end of the book that God and the church will win. That is true, but just like many historic nations, churches, and empires, you and your nation may not be around to experience it because you were negligent about the warnings written in the Bible.

We have been busy making converts, but have failed to disciple nations. As a result, though we have many converts, we are losing nations. It was a warning from the Lord. He said, "If the church in the West does not make some course corrections soon, the same thing will happen to them that happened to the early church."

In Matthew 16:18, Jesus said, "I will build My church, and the gates of hades shall not prevail against it." How then were these churches overthrown by the gates of hell? Why are we losing our Christian heritage? Why are hundreds of churches being closed every year? Kingdoms and empires that thought they would last forever cease to exist. They never thought that would happen, and neither do we. But this can happen to our society. God gave me this book to prevent that from happening. It is not God's will that these things should take place. If we take the appropriate action, what happened to those historic churches and nations will not happen to us.

Why do you go to church? Are you happy with what is going on in the church at large? Are you going to church to socialize or because you are afraid God will punish you if you do not, or to please your pastor or leader? Do you go to church to fulfill your religious duty or feel good about yourself? If you are a Christian, you go to church. That's what most of us are used to doing on Sunday morning. Afterward we go out to breakfast or lunch, and then home to watch TV and take a nap. Does that sound familiar to anyone?

But if you are a kingdom citizen, you know that when you come together as a church you assemble to exercise kingdom authority. If nothing changed when you came together, it was a fruitless exercise. There should be an improvement in the mindset of the people present or their spiritual condition. Either that or there should be a shift in the spirit world. Otherwise there is no benefit from the time spent together on a Sunday morning. If that were the case, it would have been better if we had played a game; at least the people would have benefitted from the physical exercise.

The churches in Europe and North America are still doing the same things they have done all along. They have been doing the same things, again and again, thinking someday the results they are hoping for will appear in their midst. Dear brothers and sisters and pastors, it will not happen. It's getting late and it is time to wake from our sleep.

If we do things differently and if Jesus tarries for the next ten years, I believe we can truly change the nations with the wisdom and the grace of God. That is what this book is all about. The church is a holy nation in itself: a nation within the nation you are living in (1 Peter 2:9). Jesus did not come to give us a religion, revival, a building, or a particular form of worship—He came to give us a kingdom.

> "Do not fear, little flock, for it is your Father's good pleasure to *give you the kingdom*" (Luke 12:32).

> "And *I bestow upon you a kingdom*, just as My Father bestowed *one* upon Me" (Luke 22:29).

Any nation or kingdom is only as good as the people who administer it. Most people don't know how to administer a kingdom. We are like little children whose father gave them all the wealth of this earth, but we are still crying for a little piece of candy because we do not understand the value of the wealth we already possess.

The governing influence of the church is supposed to extend to every sphere of our lives: spiritual, natural, political, and economic—every area. The church is not supposed to be excluded or separate from any part of our life. *It should all be connected.*

If there is one agency that God put on this earth to bring any necessary changes to our community and the nations, it is the church. This book is not about evangelism or church planting. This book is about how to administer the kingdom of God now, to the nations of the world and the immediate communities around us. Evangelism and church planting are by-products of that administration. God has wanted to see His kingdom established on the earth from the very beginning. When the phrase "God's kingdom on this earth" is used it is normal for a person to wonder what that looks like in the natural in this age and time.

I am very excited to bring that understanding to you from the Holy Scriptures. Establishing His kingdom does not mean overthrowing governments and taking over the geopolitical systems of this world, or building palaces and thrones and armies. It means to bring the influence of the kingdom of heaven into the kingdoms of men. It is to make known to the people of this earth that there is a God in heaven whose kingdom reigns over all.

> "Therefore know this day, and consider *it* in your heart, that the Lord Himself *is* God in heaven above and on the earth beneath; *there is* no other" (Deuteronomy 4:39).

> "And as soon as we heard *these things,* our hearts melted; neither did there remain any more courage in anyone because of you [the Israelites], for the Lord your God, He *is* God in heaven above and on earth beneath" (Joshua 2:11).

> "Then Jehoshaphat stood in the assembly of Judah and Jerusalem, in the house of the Lord, before the new court, and said: "O Lord God of our fathers, *are* You not God in heaven, and do You *not* rule over

all the kingdoms of the nations, and in Your hand *is there not* power and might, so that no one is able to withstand You? *Are* You not our God, *who* drove out the inhabitants of this land before Your people Israel, and gave it to the descendants of Abraham Your friend forever?" (2 Chronicles 20:5-7).

"The Lord has established His throne in heaven, and His kingdom rules over all" (Psalm 103:19).

"In order that the living may know that the Most High rules in the kingdom of men" (Daniel 4:17).

"Then fear came upon every soul, and many wonders and signs were done through the apostles" (Acts 2:43).

Joseph and Daniel are great examples of how, in a time and age like ours, we are supposed to administer God's kingdom in the nations we are living in. They did not overthrow the king and sit on his throne to establish God's kingdom. But, as a result of exercising the *wisdom* and *spiritual authority* God gave them, the king and all the people in the land came to recognize that there is a God in heaven and they worshiped Him.

That is what I mean by administering God's kingdom now on this earth. But it is not exclusive. There are certain times we need to remove rulers and change the laws of governments through the prayers of the church. Believe me, the *ekklesia[1]* has the power to do this, and it is in the New Testament.

In the next decade things are going to change drastically in the political arenas of the nations. There will be a tremendous

1. This refers to the governing body of the kingdom of God as a whole. Please see pages 44-45 for a complete definition.

shift in the economy and in our ways of thinking and living. Everything we believed to be true until now will be challenged. Many will fall prey to the enemy's lies, but there will be a remnant who will remain faithful to their Savior, no matter the cost. I dedicate this book to those precious ones who are going through various trails and temptations right now.

You are holding the introduction to a larger book that may have the solutions to the problems people out there are facing. We have received a kingdom, but most of us have no idea how to administer it effectively. To administer these changes, we have to be willing to learn to think differently and adopt new ways of doing things. This book will change your perception and understanding about yourself and the *ekklesia* of which you are a part. If we apply the principles outlined in this book and the one I will mention at the end of this, we will see any nation coming to Christ within ten to fifteen years of time without a single gospel crusade or healing rally.

Abraham John

Introduction

Introduction

On August 21, 2013, in the suburbs of Damascus, Syria, rockets and artillery shells containing a chemical agent called *sarin* were fired from government positions toward rebel-held villages in the eastern and southern parts of the city. This caused the death of more than 1,400 civilians, including hundreds of children.

The United Nations and the West gave the Syrian regime an ultimatum to either destroy their chemical weapons or hand them over to the U.N. If they didn't comply and allow the sites to be inspected, they would face dire consequences.

There was another element involved in Syria that could propel the situation into a possible world war if a battle broke out: the involvement of Russia. The Syrian regime that was backed by the Russians was not willing to step down and give up their power that easily. A scenario was set for a possible world war to break out at any moment.

On September 1, 2013, the president of the United States approached Congress for approval to take military action against Syria. The whole world was looking at the nation of Syria to see what would happen next. Everyone was afraid another war might break out in the Middle East, which could potentially turn into a global war because of the involvement of Russia. No one wanted that.

Five U.S. aircraft carriers were ordered to move to eastern Mediterranean waters; they were waiting for the order to fire cruise missiles into Syria to attack and destroy the chemical weapons and their plants. The U.S. Secretary of State gave the Syrian government one week to hand over its chemical weapons and allow a U.N. inspection to avoid military attack.

Time was running out. There was no positive response from the Syrian government for the first five days, but something was about to change the whole game.

A Choice to Make

On September 3, nearly seven thousand miles away from Syria, in Denver, Colorado, I was scheduled to speak. The message God gave me to share was entitled "How to Reach the World." He told me that if we are going to reach the world, we must know what it is made of.

Only a few hours were left to decide the fate of thousands of innocent people. The destruction could never be justified. Children would have lost their parents and siblings; and in addition to loss of life, hundreds of people might have become handicapped or maimed. The devastation would have been horrific.

There I was, preparing to preach about how to reach the world, when most of the world was in fear and turmoil because another war was about to break forth. I had two options before me: the first was to preach a nice sermon to please the crowd, pray for them at the end, and many would come and tell me how wonderful the sermon was.

But I had another option before me: to do something in the spirit about what was imminent in Syria, for the thousands of people who had not yet heard the gospel of Christ and the salvation He offers. They could go to hell and we wouldn't even know they ever existed.

> **There I was, preparing to preach about how to reach the world, when most of the world was in fear and turmoil because another war was about to break forth.**

Ekklesia is a Greek term that describes the governing body of the church as a whole, the church universal. The Holy Spirit, the Governor of the *Ekklesia*, stepped in and told me to lead the *ekklesia* in prayer for what was going on in Syria, so there would not be another war. The Bible says God's house shall be called a house of prayer for all nations.

We prayed fervently that night. We prayed and declared that there would not be another war in Syria. We exercised our God-given authority to intervene to save the lives of thousands of innocent people. Something dramatic happened in the world of international politics within the following eight hours. The Syrian regime consented to the demands of the United Nations for the destruction of their chemical weapons and allowed them to inspect the sites. It was a temporary victory, and as I write, the problems are still raging. They need our continued prayers.

I am not saying the above result came just because of *our* prayers. There might have been thousands of other members

> **What could happen in our country if believers spent at least a fraction of their Sunday morning services praying for their communities and nations?**

of the *ekklesia* around the world who were also praying. The reason I mention the above incident is to show what our prayers could do if the *ekklesia* really prayed. What could happen in our country if believers spent at least a fraction of their Sunday morning services praying for their communities and nations?

Have We Missed Our Purpose?

I know that many are waiting for the rapture to take place. Could it be possible that we miss God and what He has for us now—like many of the first century Jewish people missed their Messiah—because we're looking for the wrong thing? They were considered the most spiritual people of their time. I strongly believe the season the entire world has been waiting centuries for has come upon us. Perhaps we can't see the forest through the trees.

Would God give Jesus all authority in heaven and on earth, and He in turn give it to the *ekklesia* if He does not want us to use that authority right here and now? Would He want us to use it after the rapture instead? I don't think so. Is it God's will for the majority of the people alive today to go to hell? That is probably what would happen if the rapture were to take place right now.

The time has come for God's children to take their place on this earth before Jesus comes back. There is one Scripture that is quoted more times from the Old Testament in the New Testament than any other verse. It's not about getting born again, the rapture, or prayer for revival. In this verse the Father is telling His Son to sit at His right hand until He makes His enemies His footstool. It is quoted seven times in the New Testament. I began to wonder why that particular Scripture was quoted more times than any other and I believe there is a definite reason for it. *In fact, this verse is quoted in the first message Peter preached that was the catalyst for the New Testament church.*

> "For David did not ascend into the heavens, but he says himself: 'The Lord said to my Lord, "Sit at My right hand, till I make Your enemies Your footstool" ' " (Acts 2:34-35).

We do not yet see that Jesus' enemies have been made His footstool in the practical sense. When will this happen, and who is going to do the job? Through Jesus' death and resurrection He received all authority in heaven and on earth. In turn, He gave that authority to His church. Now the church has to exercise that authority to bring His enemies to His footstool. He is waiting for this to happen so He can return to the earth.

> "But this Man, after He had offered one sacrifice for sins forever, sat down at the right hand of God, *from that time waiting till His enemies are made His footstool"* (Hebrews 10:12-13).

If someone on TV tells you that Jesus is going to come next year, please don't sell your belongings and pack your stuff. He is not coming until the church overcomes this world and His enemies are made His footstool. How is the Father going to accomplish this task for His Son? In this battle, the Son is not going to fight to make the enemy His footstool. He already finished His work on the cross and received the right to sit at His Father's right hand. The most important part of those two verses is the Son being asked to "*sit till*" the Father makes His enemies His footstool. And the Son has been sitting and waiting for that to happen. Believe it or not, He is not going to do anything else until that takes place.

Neither is the Father going to come to this earth to fight against the enemy. There is only one way this can be accomplished and that is through the *ekklesia*, the body of Christ on the earth today, under the direction of the Holy Spirit. You and I are part of that body, and subsequently part of the battle to make His enemies His footstool. This book is all about equipping the saints to do just that. If this is to happen, the current church needs to make a U-turn. Fast.

How is the *ekklesia* going to accomplish this task? For this to happen we need to know what the *ekklesia* is all about. Why did Jesus leave us on this earth? Is it to sing to Him? If so, why didn't He ask anyone to sing to Him while He was here? Did God ask Adam to sing to Him? We have been misinformed about our mission and purpose. For too long we have been deceived and robbed of our inheritance and our rights as the children of Almighty God.

When the *ekklesia* exercises her rightful authority and brings Jesus' enemies to His footstool, He in turn will deliver the kingdom to God the Father and then the end will come.

> "Then *comes* the end, when He delivers the kingdom to God the Father, when He puts an end

22

to all rule and all authority and power. For He must reign till He has put all enemies under His feet" (1 Corinthians 15:24-25).

The kingdoms of this world must become the kingdoms of our Lord and of His Christ (Revelation 11:15).

A New Era

With the year 2000, we entered a new era in the kingdom movement led by apostles. The church has yet to embrace this. Most are still trying to revamp the past season. The church as a whole

> **With the year 2000, we entered a new era in the kingdom movement led by apostles.**

is not ready to receive apostolic ministry. When apostles come they don't come with a little "God loves you" message or motivational speech. Instead they come with apostolic doctrines, which for most are difficult to receive. We need to pray for the church to be ready to receive the ministry of an apostle. This may require a great deal of restructuring in the way things are done.

The Kingdom or Apostolic Age has three major characteristics. One is a greater manifestation of God's wisdom and authority through His people; the second is increased persecution against Christians; and the third is the advancement of the kingdom in the midst of that persecution.

If you look at the early church—or anyone who made a difference for God—you will see these characteristics manifested in their lives. But the good news is that God's kingdom and His ekklesia always prevailed if they remained faithful to their Commander-in-Chief. People like Joseph, Daniel, Paul, and the brethren of the early church existed and grew in very hostile environments. There is something amazing about the kingdom of God: When it is hard pressed, it will bring to nothing everything that opposes it. I like what Jesus said about His kingdom, "Therefore I say to you, the kingdom of God will be taken from you and given to a nation bearing the fruits of it. And whoever falls on this stone will be broken; but on whomever it falls, it will grind him to powder" (Matthew 21:44).

Throughout the Bible and history, God raised up certain people and nations to make known His greatness, wisdom, and power to the rest of the earth. The Bible tells why God raised up Pharaoh, the king of Egypt, "For the Scripture says to the Pharaoh, 'For this very purpose I have raised you up, that I may show My power in you, and that My name may be declared in all the earth' " (Romans 9:17).

Jesus said, "My house shall be called a house of prayer for all nations" (Mark 11:17). Today in our churches, we have made what is most important the least important, and the least important things have become the most prominent part of our program. If we spent twenty minutes singing, and took just five minutes of that to pray as a congregation, what would God do through that church? Even when we pray, we spend most of the time asking God for things He has already given us. So, we pray amiss.

Just before the year 2000, most of the world was caught up (the church included) with Y2K. They thought the world was going to end and Jesus was going to come in that year. Y2K came and went and we are still here. People constantly make claims like that, saying Jesus is going to come this year. I asked the Lord why such things happen and He reminded me that He said that many would rise and say they have found the Messiah.

> "'Then if anyone says to you, 'Look, here *is* the Christ!' or 'There!' do not believe *it.* For false Christs and false prophets will rise and show great signs and wonders to deceive, if possible, even the elect'" (Matthew 24:23-24).

In fact, this will increase in the days ahead. God told us not to be deceived by those people. The reason these false prophets arise is to deceive the church in order to keep her ineffective and disengaged. When they hear Jesus is going to come this year, many people become fearful and do not engage in what is going on in their community and nation. They seclude themselves and wait for the rapture to take place. They give the devil plenty of freedom to do whatever he wants to do, while the church just watches and waits.

> **The reason these false prophets arise is to deceive the church in order to keep her ineffective and disengaged.**

Where Is the Everlasting Kingdom?

Vast numbers of people have lost trust in the church. The American church is becoming more secular than Christian, and Europe has become one of the least Christian continents on earth. Have you ever wondered why such things happen? It is not because great revivals did not take place in these regions. To most people in the world, Christianity is just another religion with rules, regulations, and rituals. Jesus never intended His kingdom on earth to be known as a religion. The devil knew that if he could bring Christianity down to the level of a religion, it would lose its very essence and people would stay away from it.

Why would someone who belongs to one religion change to another? In some parts of the world people have changed their religion to gain better material or social benefits, but their lives cannot be used to build God's kingdom on earth because they never had a true revelation of who God is and how His kingdom operates. So, when someone else offers them better benefits, they will change their religion again. This is happening in India right now as I write this book.

The devil has a counterfeit for everything God has and does. In fact, he has a false church operating now. Unfortunately, many so-called Christians are part of that pseudo-church. The devil also does better social and charitable works than most Christians. Additionally, he has people in authority in governments and businesses all over the world to execute his will and purpose.

You might be wondering if I am a propagator of "kingdom now" or "dominion theology." I am not. I am a kingdom *forever* guy because God's kingdom is everlasting and His dominion has no end (Luke 1:33). He reigns forever. Dimensions and manifestations of this vary according to how the people on the earth respond.

In the Old and New Testaments, God used His people to administer His kingdom, and He has given us the power and authority to do the same. The whole world is waiting for the manifestation of the sons of God (Romans 8:19).

If you are part of that end-time army of God, what I write in this book will bear witness in your spirit. I would like to ask you a favor. Just like the believers in Berea did, please refer to the Holy Scriptures to see that what I am sharing here lines up with the Word of God. I also request that you not reject a truth just because it is not popular. Are you ready?

Chapter 1: The *Ekklesia*

Chapter 1: The *Ekklesia*

"The mystery which has been hidden from ages and from generations, but now has been revealed to His saints" (Colossians 1:26).

The *ekklesia* is one of the mysteries that was hidden in the heart of God from eternity past and has been revealed to us in this day and age through His apostles and prophets. Believe it or not, we are part of that era that every prophet and saint we admire in the Old Testament looked forward to seeing. They yearned to see and live in this day and age. A couple of them—by faith—grabbed the grace we are enjoying now, brought it into reality, and lived in it. People like Abraham and David are examples.

A Matter of Perspective

The church we see today is like the poem called "The Blind Men and the Elephant"

> The *ekklesia* is one of the mysteries that was hidden in the heart of God from eternity past and has been revealed to us in this day and age.

31

by John Godfrey Saxe. These blind men had never seen anything before, let alone an elephant. They had heard much from other people about this humongous animal but could not really imagine exactly what it would look like. To end their curiosity, they decided to go and explore for themselves. They would "feel" how an elephant *looks* so they could put together the pieces of their imagination and finally "see" the elephant.

One of them touched the leg of the elephant and thought it felt like a tree. He said the elephant looked like a tree. The second touched the trunk of the elephant and came back saying it looked like a snake. The third touched the tail of the elephant and thought the elephant was like a rope. The fourth touched its ear and returned saying it looked like a big fan. The fifth touched the stomach of the elephant and claimed the elephant was like a wall. The sixth man happened to touch the elephant's tusk, so he told the others it was like a spear.

If we take just one of their reports as the ultimate truth, how accurate will the description of an elephant be? To be honest, an elephant is *like* everything explained above. But if you took only one of their descriptions and came to a conclusion, it would be wrong and not an accurate picture of an elephant. An elephant is not a tree, snake, rope, fan, wall, or spear. Only when we put all of these perceptions together will we get an idea of what an elephant really looks like.

The last stanza of the poem reads:

> So oft in theologic wars,
> The disputants, I ween,
> Rail on in utter ignorance

Of what each other mean,
And prate about an Elephant
Not one of them has seen.[2]

For many centuries the church has been arguing and fighting about particular doctrines and traditions. That fight birthed various denominations and sects, each one specializing in different truths or aspects of the church. The church is a multi-faceted organism. Many have tried to "singlify" its objective through the centuries and they all went astray in their portrayal of the church.

Some say the church's focus should be on evangelism and saving sinners. Others say it should be on power, healing, and miracles. Still others say the focus should be on loving others, feeding the hungry, taking care of orphans, and helping the poor. Many believe our purpose is to worship and teach the Word of God. There may be other concepts and descriptions of the church that come to your mind, such as the building and the clergy. It could be faith and prosperity, grace, holiness, or revival.

Just like those blind men missed grasping the full understanding of an elephant, we as believers have missed what God's purpose for the church is, and thus we remain ineffective in our nations. The church is the only hope for the nations. Only the church can offer real solutions to the problems we are facing in our world today. It is time to put all the pieces together, break down the walls that separate us, and embrace one another in the unity of the Spirit—not in the unity of our perceptions.

---

2. Saxe, John Godfrey. "The Blind Men and the Elephant." Public domain.

Jesus Didn't Teach Much about the Church

Jesus mentioned the word *church* only twice in the four Gospels. That shocked me! If Jesus came to establish His church on the earth, why didn't He teach about it more? Why didn't He teach His disciples about church administration, homiletics (the science of preaching), building funds, church picnics, revivals, worship, and choir? They would be the ones leading the church once it began, after all.

For almost twenty years of my life I was focused on evangelism, church planting, training pastors, and taking care of orphans. I was not happy with the results.

> **Jesus mentioned the word *church* only twice in the four Gospels.**

My mindset was that if I could win more people to Christ and if there were more Christians in a nation, it would be transformed to heaven on earth. Then I realized that the kingdom of darkness was thriving in the nations with a Christian majority! I went to God with my problem.

That's when God began to give me revelation and insight. Though I received the revelation of the kingdom of God and preached it, the people who listened to those messages were not able to receive the revelation because they were drenched in a *church mentality* instead of a *kingdom mindset*.

For most of the people I trained, planting another church or baptizing another convert was the most important part of their agenda. They were not concerned about God establishing His kingdom on this earth. When Jesus taught us to pray, His first priority was summed up in this statement, "Let Your kingdom come and Your will be done on earth as it

34

is in heaven." He did not ask us to pray, "Let another church be planted on the other side of the street" or "Take us all to heaven as soon as possible." No. Jesus never asked anyone to *plant* or *start* a church.

So what is the purpose of the church? What did God intend in His heart when He thought of the church? If a company sends its representative overseas to train people about a new product they are planning to launch, that representative will explain everything about that product so their employees in that country will be ready to market it effectively. That sounds right, doesn't it?

Get a Glimpse of God's Perspective

God operates from a different perspective. Imagine His kingdom as the *company* that was launching the product and the church as the *product*. Jesus was teaching and training his disciples about the company and its method of operation more than about the product. He wanted them to become familiar with the company and its Owner before becoming too passionate about its product because only if an employee knew the purpose, values, and the mission of the company, would he understand why it was launching a particular product and then be able to explain it to others. The product represents the company and is intended to fulfill its vision and mission.

Jesus Taught about the Kingdom

Although the church was going to be the greatest enterprise God ever began on this earth, Jesus, who is the Head of the church, only mentioned it twice in His entire recorded preaching and teaching. On the other hand, He mentioned His kingdom more than a hundred times in the four Gospels.

> **He (Jesus) mentioned His kingdom more than a hundred times in the four Gospels.**

Jesus wanted His disciples to become familiar with how His kingdom operated. He wanted to create a kingdom mindset in them before they ever got to do anything with His church. The church is here to administer God's kingdom, but if its leaders don't know what the kingdom is and what it is made of, how can they administer it?

If Jesus' only intent for starting His church on the earth was to get a bunch of people saved and take them to heaven, then why did He spend so much time preaching and teaching about the kingdom of God? He could have just saved all that for when we got to heaven if there was no specific purpose or benefit to us knowing about His kingdom here on earth. If all He wanted was a choir in heaven, why would He create this planet Earth and put us here, allowing us to go through all this turmoil? Why would He allow His Son to endure what He endured? He could have just created us and put us in heaven in the first place! A religious spirit has deceived us for a very long time regarding our purpose personally and the purpose of the church as a whole.

I do not intend to condemn or diminish what the church is already doing today, but I would like to add an important missing and neglected element to its present program. Without it the church won't be as effective as it should be, regardless of what program, teaching, or even miracles we may have. God's purpose is to restore that kingdom mindset to His people who have been drenched in a church mentality for hundreds of years. There are many who are weary of it and can't wait to be part of a change.

Following are my intentions for writing this book:

◆ To train church members to be kingdom citizens

◆ To train believers to live as sons and daughters of God on this earth

◆ To equip kingdom citizens to exercise their rights and authority to administer His kingdom in the communities and the nations in which they are living

◆ To deliver the church from a religion, rapture, and revival mentality to a kingdom mindset

◆ To communicate that there is still hope for the West, but that hope is in the church

"I Will Build My *Ekklesia*"

The Greek word used for the church in the New Testament is *ekklesia*. What exactly does it mean? What picture came to the disciples' minds when Jesus mentioned the church to them for the first time? The word *ekklesia* in Greek means, "called out ones." [3] Called out from what and for what purpose?

When Jesus mentioned the church, the disciples did not take Him aside and ask Him for further direction like they did when He taught them how to pray. When we think of the

---

3. Thayer and Smith. "Greek Lexicon entry for *ekklesia*." "The NAS New Testament Greek Lexicon." 1999. Web.

church today, we think of a building with a cross on the top, or we picture a gathering of people singing or listening to a preacher. I wonder what came to the minds of the disciples when they heard the word *church* for the first time.

When Jesus referred to the church, He never mentioned worship or singing or offerings or helping poor people. He mentioned three things: (1) the fact that He would build it, (2) the idea that there was a battle going on, and (3) that the church would reconcile relationships.

If the establishing of the church was such an important enterprise, why didn't He give more explanation about it? Why didn't He train the disciples about how to conduct a service or take an effective offering to meet their budget for different ministries? There are two reasons Jesus did not do that. First of all, He did not come with the purpose of revealing the management of a church. Instead His message was about the kingdom of God. He came to reveal that kingdom and give back to us what we lost because of Adam's sin.

The second reason Jesus didn't teach about the church was that the revelation of the church that we are part of was to be given to Paul. It was through him that God chose to reveal the mystery of the church and how it is supposed to operate on the earth.

> **Every kingdom on this earth had a *church* or *ekklesia* that administered its policies and rules.**

Some people think the church did not begin until His resurrection. That is not true. The church has been on this earth ever since the kingdom of God began to operate here. Every kingdom on this earth had a *church or ekklesia* that administered its policies and rules. Without a church, a kingdom cannot operate and without a kingdom, a church will not survive. I will show you that from the Scriptures in the following pages. The concept of the church was revealed in the Bible and throughout history in both the political and spiritual sense long before the New Testament church began.

Called Out

> "This is he, that was *in the church in the wilderness* with the angel which spake to him in the Mount Sinai, and with our fathers: who received the lively oracles to give unto us" (Acts 7:38 KJV).

From this verse we understand that what might have come to the disciples' heart when Jesus mentioned the word *ekklesia* was a picture of the people of Israel in the wilderness; the same Greek word is used in the above verse to describe them. What was significant about the people of Israel in the wilderness? What did they do and how did they live as God's *ekklesia,* the called out ones? If we study their lives and the way God dealt with them, and how they handled their internal problems, we will get somewhat of an understanding about the church in the New Testament. Paul said that everything they went through was for our example (1 Corinthians 10:6, 11).

The Israelites were *called out* by God (from Egypt) to be a special kingdom of priests (Exodus 19:6) through whom He would accomplish His purpose on earth. The church today is also the called out ones and royal priesthood (1 Peter 2:9). Whatever they experienced in the physical realm, we experience in the spiritual. Whatever power and authority they exercised in the physical world, we have over both the spiritual and the natural world.

God is a king and He has a kingdom He wants to establish on the earth. That is His ultimate plan and objective. *Everything He does* is geared toward accomplishing that one purpose and nothing else. He wants to reveal His wisdom, glory, and power to the people on earth as well as to the principalities and powers in the heavenly places (Ephesians 3:10).

Another reason the disciples did not question Jesus about the church when He mentioned it was because they were familiar with the concept of *ekklesia* from a political perspective. They knew Jesus is a king and that every king needs an ekklesia. It was a political term used in the Greek world and was never used to address a group of people who worshiped, preached, or sang. It was used to represent a group of men who were called out from among the people by a king or government to administer the political, judicial, economic, and social affairs of the people.

> **Jesus is the king and He has a kingdom so He needs an *ekklesia* to govern the affairs of His kingdom. That is why He started the church.**

Every king and kingdom had an *ekklesia* that governed its affairs. Jesus added a spiritual dimension to His kingdom when He said, "I will build my church" (Matthew 16:18), because His kingdom is a spiritual kingdom. Jesus is the king and He has a kingdom so He needs an *ekklesia* to govern the affairs of His kingdom. That is why He started the church.

The church is a multi-faceted organism and it has a very complex purpose and responsibility. Worship, preaching and teaching of the Word, reaching the lost, missions, prayer groups, praying for the sick, helping the poor and the widows, children's ministry, offerings, various types of ministries and classes, are all only various aspects and duties of a local church. But what is the main purpose of the church?

The Church Should Help You Solve Your Problems

When Jesus mentioned the church the first time, it was in the context of a political confrontation. It was a confrontation between two kingdoms: His church and the gates of hades. In this case the two kingdoms are spiritual kingdoms. They are the kingdom of God and the kingdom of darkness.

> "And I also say to you that you are Peter, and on this rock I will build My church, and the gates of Hades shall not prevail against it" (Matthew 16:18).

Jesus refers to the church as something He builds to withstand the operation of hades, or the powers of darkness. The above verse refers to a spiritual battle — one the church needs to be prepared to fight.

The second time Jesus mentioned the church, it was in reference to addressing or solving the relational (social) problems people have.

> "Moreover if your brother sins against you, go and tell him his fault between you and him alone. If he hears you, you have gained your brother. But if he will not hear, take with you one or two more, that

'by the mouth of two or three witnesses every word may be established.' And if he refuses to hear them, tell *it* to the church. But if he refuses even to hear the church, let him be to you like a heathen and a tax collector" (Matthew 18:15-17).

This verse refers to the church as a place where judicial or social problems are solved. When a person has an offense against another and they cannot find a solution by themselves, they are to bring it before the church to solve it. Jesus did not say when two people have problems, they need to go to church and worship. No, they are to *tell it to the ekklesia*. If the church was a building, could we tell our problem to a building? But the church is not a building; it is a group of people. And if the person refuses to *hear the church* (that group of people), let him be to you like a heathen and a tax collector.

The church needs to administer the kingdom of God and govern the affairs of men and women in society. When two people have problems between them, Jesus did not say to go to the court system of the world, but to the church, a group of people appointed by God to administer His kingdom (Matthew 18:15-17). Even Paul admonished the Corinthian church to not go to a court of law against another believer. He asked the church to solve the issue.

"Dare any of you, having a matter against another, go to law before the unrighteous, and not before the saints? *Do you not know that the saints will judge the world?* And if the world will be judged by you, are you unworthy to judge the smallest matters? Do you not know that we shall judge angels? *How much more, things that pertain to this life?*" (1 Corinthians 6:1-3).

When do you think we will be judging the world and angels? I was taught that we are going to heaven to sing. Paul is saying that we are going to judge the world and the angels, so how much more should we judge things that pertain to this life

> **Each time Jesus mentioned the church, He referred to a governing body, not a place of worship.**

now? When the Israelites had a judicial, social, or spiritual problem they brought it before their leaders. They did not go before the Gentiles to get help. That is the way the church is supposed to function too.

Each time Jesus mentioned the church, He referred to a governing body, not a place of worship. He referred to a group of people who were assigned to exercise authority to solve problems both in *the spiritual* and in *the natural* world. In the political world of those days, the *ekklesia* was a group of people who were called out—or selected—from the general public to govern the affairs of a kingdom or a nation.

The disciples knew that every king had an *ekklesia* in his kingdom that governed his affairs. That's why they kept asking Him when He was going to set up His kingdom on the earth. They wanted to sit and rule with Him (Matthew 20:21; Acts 1:6). When we read the gospel of Matthew, we notice that it was after Jesus said He will build His *ekklesia* that the mother of James and John came with the request for her sons to sit on His right and on His left in His kingdom (Matthew 20:20-21). They wanted to be part of His *ekklesia*, the governing body of His kingdom, but they only understood the natural aspect of the term. That's what they were familiar with at that time. The spiritual revelation of His kingdom or *ekklesia* came to them later.

Definitions for *Ekklesia*

Here are a series of definitions of the word *ekklesia* by respected Greek scholars. Please read them with an open mind.

> Liddell and Scott define *ekklesia* as "an assembly of citizens summoned by the crier, the legislative assembly."[4]

> Thayer's *Lexicon* says, "an assembly of the people convened at the public place of council for the purpose of deliberating."[5]

> Trench gives the meaning as, "the lawful assembly in a free Greek city of all those possessed of the rights of citizenship, for the transaction of public affairs."[6]

> Seyffert's *Dictionary* states "The assembly of the people, which in Greek cities had the power of final decision in public affairs."[7]

4. Liddell, Henry George, and Robert Scott. A Greek-English Lexicon. Oxford: University Press, 1855. 206.

5. Thayer, Joseph Henry, Carl Ludwig Wilibald Grimm, Christian Gottlob Wilke, and James Strong. Thayer's Greek-English Lexicon of the New Testament: Coded with the Numbering System from Strong's Exhaustive Concordance of the Bible. Peabody, MA: Hendrickson Publishers, 1896. 196.

6. Trench, Richard Chenevix. Synonyms of the New Testament. Grand Rapids: W.B. Eerdmans Pub., 1948. 1, 2.

7. Seyffert, Oskar, Henry Nettleship, and John Edwin Sandys. A Dictionary of Classical Antiquities, Mythology, Religion, Literature, Art. New York: Meridian Books, 1956. 202, 203.

As you read this book, keep these definitions in your heart concerning the church. From here onward when you hear the word *church*, try to envision a "legislative assembly" instead of a building, people singing, or pastors preaching. The definition God gave me for the *church* is, "the governing body of the kingdom of God on this earth" or "a group of people who are called by God to administer the kingdom of God on this earth." Try to keep those definitions in your heart.

The picture that comes to your mind when you hear the word *church* is actually very important because that picture forms the perception and understanding you have of the church. Most of the time it's not a biblical perspective, but one formed by the religious culture or a

> **In the New Testament, people used to go to the temple—not to church. The church *met* in the temple or houses. *They* were the church.**

particular tradition we grew up in. We say things like, "I grew up in church," or "I go to church," or "there was a special meeting in church." In the New Testament, people never used such terms. They used to go to the temple—not to church. The church *met* in the temple or houses. *They* were the church.

I want to make it very clear that the purpose of the church is not to be a charitable organization under any earthly government to take care of orphans and to feed the poor and widows. That's just one aspect of the ministry every local church must do; it's not the sole purpose. What do you think was in Jesus' mind when He used the word *church*? Was He thinking of a building where a group of people would come together to sing and hear someone preach on a Sunday morning? I don't think so.

The church is also not a non-profit organization that receives grants and subsidies from the government for its ministers or activities. It is not an entity to which you can donate money and claim it on your year-end tax return. The government allowed that because it was the church that was once entirely responsible for education and for taking care of the poor and the sick in our nation. But things have changed.

I will be using different phrases and words to express the concept of the church throughout this book. I will be using verses from the Bible multiple times to emphasize certain truths. When I refer to the church, I am never referring to a building or a particular denomination, sect, or group. The church is the body of Christ on the earth. I do not belong to any particular sect, group, or denomination. I belong to Christ and I am a member of His body and an ambassador of His kingdom to the earth. I have been sent to equip the body of Christ to administer His kingdom on the earth so that He can return.

If the church is here to administer God's kingdom, how do we do it in a practical sense? If God is making a "kingdom move" on the earth today, how does each believer take part in it? I am confident that as you read this book you will find the answers to those questions.

Additionally, I pray that God will open the eyes of your understanding to see everything He intended to do for His church and through His church on this earth. He is waiting for His body to catch up with His agenda and prioritize their lives according to His purpose. In Him we live and move and have our being (Acts 17:28).

Chapter 2: The Gospel of the Kingdom

Chapter 2: The Gospel of the Kingdom

"And this gospel of the kingdom will be preached in all the world as a witness to all the nations, and then the end will come" (Matthew 24:14).

What type of gospel did Jesus and the apostles preach in the first century? Why did Jesus start the church? Did He start it so we can help people get born again? If so, why did He not train or talk much about that? (He talked about being born again when He spoke to Nicodemus, but at no other time.) Did He want people to worship Him? If so, why did He never ask anyone to sing to Him, nor have a choir practice with His disciples? Why did He only talk about the church as a body two times during three-and-a-half years of ministry on the earth? And in comparison, why did He speak about the gospel of the kingdom more than a hundred and twenty times? His teaching about the kingdom was vitally important, so He spoke of it more than anything else.

> **Matthew wrote his gospel to prove to the world that Jesus is the king, to introduce us to His kingdom.**

49

KINGDOM MANDATE

Have you ever wondered why God put the gospel of Matthew as the first book of the New Testament? He had a specific reason behind it. Each gospel is written to address a different group of people and to reveal a main character trait of Jesus and also a different aspect of His kingdom. Matthew wrote his gospel to prove to the world that Jesus is the king, to introduce us to His kingdom, and to show the Jewish people that He is the rightful heir to the throne of David. In it He revealed the kingdom mandate to us.

God wants the New Testament reader to know that with Jesus' coming, He started a new era of His kingdom here on earth. God wants us to look at the rest of the New Testament and this age with a kingdom mindset. Matthew talks about the gospel of the kingdom.

"But seek *first* the kingdom of God and His righteousness, and all these things shall be added to you" (Matthew 6:33). What did Jesus mean by telling us to seek His kingdom *first*?

In Christianity today, a person hears more about worship, tongues, the coming rapture, revival, fire, hell, anointing, prosperity, grace, healing, miracles, and a lot of other things, before they ever hear anything about the kingdom. I did not hear anything about the kingdom until I was twenty years into my Christian life and I was already in ministry! And I was a Pentecostal! Can you believe that? In the disciples' case, the first message and the last message (before His ascension) that they heard from the mouth of Jesus was about the kingdom. It is because we have lost that as our focus that the church is not functioning the way it should.

Why did Jesus ask us to seek His kingdom first? It is because He knows that until we discover His kingdom we will not be fully satisfied. Man was created to live in His kingdom. Without His kingdom, even if we live in a mansion, we will feel like something is missing deep inside. We have this instinct in us to keep pursuing luxury and comfort but luxury will not satisfy us, regardless of how much of it we have. It is the longing of our spirit to find its home, but many misunderstand it and run after the pleasures of this world instead. So, the first thing He wants us to seek and find is His kingdom. Once we have it and learn to live in it, we have everything. Though in the natural we may have much or little, our spirit will feel at home.

Once you discover God's kingdom and learn to live in it, you will realize that everything you need is in His kingdom. There is joy in His kingdom. You may have lost your joy and depend on something of this world to bring happiness instead, but once you discover the kingdom you learn to tap into the joy that is in it. Kingdom joy is not based on what you possess or what you do. It comes from knowing the King, His kingdom, His love and plan for your life. God has made all of the resources, wealth, and wisdom that are in heaven available to us through Jesus Christ. We need to tap into them by faith. The only way to live in His kingdom is by faith and trusting in Him moment by moment.

The Gospel of the Kingdom

Among the four Gospels, it is only in the gospel of Matthew that Jesus talks about the church. God wants us to see the entire age of the church and the New Testament through a kingdom lens.

It is the book of Matthew that includes the twelve parables that reveal the mysteries of the kingdom of heaven. It is Matthew that talks about the culture and decrees and laws of the kingdom of God. It is in Matthew that Jesus said, "And this *gospel of the kingdom* will be preached in all the world as a witness to all the nations, and then the end will come" (Matthew 24:14).

Why the gospel of the kingdom? There are many types of gospels being preached today (2 Corinthians 11:4; Galatians 1:8); each denomination has their own version of the gospel message. I have not yet heard a group that preaches the gospel of the kingdom who has a full understanding about how a kingdom operates. That's why the world and the church are in the condition they are in today. We have been preaching every other kind of gospel: Pentecostal gospel, Baptist gospel, prosperity gospel, full gospel, half gospel, etc.: everything except the gospel of the kingdom. The following chart will show you some of the different kinds of gospels that are being preached today.

Humanistic Gospel/ Man-Centered Gospel	Religious Gospel/Gospel of Salvation	Legalistic Gospel	Gospel of the Kingdom/Gospel of the Lord Jesus Christ
Focuses on self	Focus on a self-made religious god and formed by the traditions of men	Worships the Law	Connected by an intimate relationship with Father, Son, and the Holy Spirit
Focuses on material blessings	Focuses on the power of God	Judges and criticizes one another/ compares to see who is better	Focuses on love and relationships

Humanistic Gospel/ Man-Centered Gospel	Religious Gospel/Gospel of Salvation	Legalistic Gospel	Gospel of the Kingdom/Gospel of the Lord Jesus Christ
It's all about what you can have now, no spiritual perception of what is happening around them	Focuses on what you will have in heaven and spiritualizes everything.	There is nothing here and not much in heaven	Maintains balance between suffering and blessings on this earth
Preaches about all the blessed saints in the Bible	Enforces suffering for eternal glory and preaches about the suffering of the saints in the Bible	Believes all the people God used were perfect	Believes in both suffering and blessing
Cheap grace	Very little grace	No grace at all	Sound and balanced revelation of grace
Serves money/ mammon	Glorifies poverty	Nothing to enjoy on this side of heaven	All needs are met
Self-empowerment	Self-rejection	Self-deceived	Self-denial
Self-righteous	Righteousness by good works	Righteousness by obeying the law	Righteousness of God by faith
Personal success/achievements	Does not believe in success	Does not care about success	Doing and fulfilling the will/ purpose of God

Humanis-tic Gospel/ Man-Centered Gospel	Religious Gospel/Gospel of Salvation	Legalistic Gospel	Gospel of the Kingdom/Gospel of the Lord Jesus Christ
Focuses on prosperity	Focuses on salvation, heaven, and hell.	Focuses on obeying the Ten Command-ments	Focuses on God and His kingdom
Lives to make money	Lives to be religious	Lives to appear spiritual	Lives to glorify the Father
Thinks they are the best	Live with an 'I am nothing, just dust' attitude	Makes up and adds new rules	Lives to make Him great
Focuses on independence	Focuses on servitude	Lives to be served	Lives to serve others
Calls sin a weakness	Covers up sins	Slave to sin	Dead to sin
Gets rid of the cross	The cross is too heavy to carry	Adds more crosses	Carries the cross daily
Anything and everything goes	Lives in fear of being punished by God	Has no mercy at all—for self or others	Trusts in God's mercy and forgives from the heart
Marked by perfectionism	Trying to be perfected in the flesh	Looks perfect outwardly	Focuses on the heart
Lives to do "big" things/ Dream "big" philosophy	Lives to preach	Lives to observe rules	Lives to administer the kingdom of God
Trusts an individualistic holiness	Most holy people	Believes they are the only true saints and keepers of the faith	Trusts in Christ's holiness

Humanistic Gospel/ Man-Centered Gospel	Religious Gospel/Gospel of Salvation	Legalistic Gospel	Gospel of the Kingdom/Gospel of the Lord Jesus Christ
Denies reality	Have zeal without knowledge	Have no power	No sickness, poverty, or curse
Exalts self	Devoted to following the traditions of men	Focused on being right	Led by the Spirit—moment by moment
"Will" worship	Follows form of religion	Worships in the flesh	Worships God in spirit and truth
Entertains and builds up the souls of men	Doesn't smile at church	It is a sin to be joyful	Joy of the Lord is our strength
Always buys the most expensive	Don't buy anything/ Lives with poverty mindset	Always buys the cheapest	Lives content with little or an abundance
Theme of most songs is, I, Me, and Mine	Theme of most songs is the coming of Jesus and life in heaven	Theme of most songs is suffering and the sweet by and by	Theme of most songs is exalting, magnifying, and worshiping the King
Gives the list to God and tells Him what to do	Always says, "If it is God's will."	Always has a condition to meet	Lives as a son to do the will of the Father, waits on His direction.
Sees things in the light of the blessings they can get	Sees things in the light of hell	Sees things in the light of observing rituals	Sees things in the light of eternity

KINGDOM MANDATE

Humanistic Gospel/ Man-Centered Gospel	Religious Gospel/Gospel of Salvation	Legalistic Gospel	Gospel of the Kingdom/Gospel of the Lord Jesus Christ
Joy based on circumstances	Looking forward to having joy in heaven	Can never do enough. Miserable day and night	Rejoice in the Lord always
Acceptance based on achievements	Acceptance based on religious works	Acceptance based on performance	Accepted based on love of Christ; adopted as His children
Lives to please self	Lives by the fear of man	Lives to please people	God is already pleased with us; obeys Him out of love
Accumulates material wealth	Never have enough	Pretends to be blessed	Receives inheritance and manages it wisely
Man is the center of the universe	Rituals are the center of the universe	Everything centered around the Law	God is the center of the universe.
Believes everything was created for us.	Believes man was created to worship God	Believes man was created to obey God	Man was created to have fellowship with God, which leads to dominion
Believes in the great promises of the Bible that have personal benefits	Has Great Commission as priority	Has Ten Commandments as priority	Has greatest commandment as priority
You are the boss	Lives as a pilgrim/orphan	Lives as a slave	Lives as a son and becomes a father to many

Humanis-tic Gospel/ Man-Centered Gospel	Religious Gospel/Gospel of Salvation	Legalistic Gospel	Gospel of the Kingdom/Gospel of the Lord Jesus Christ
I can do it myself	Lives in the past or in a futuristic attitude	Only doom, gloom, and despair	Lives based on the revelation of "It is finished."

It is time to start doing what is right and what we are really called to do. We need to preach the gospel that Jesus preached and commanded us to preach.

> "Then Jesus went about all the cities and villages, teaching in their synagogues, preaching the gospel of the kingdom, and healing every sickness and every disease among the people" (Matthew 9:35).

> "Now after John was put in prison, Jesus came to Galilee, preaching the gospel of the kingdom of God" (Mark 1:14).

Seeing the World through a Kingdom Lens

Jesus wanted His disciples to have a kingdom perspective, a kingdom worldview. He wanted them to see the world through that kingdom paradigm before they got to do anything with the church. To prepare them, day and night He taught, preached, and trained them about the kingdom and how it operated. Therefore, God in His sovereignty ordained Matthew to be the first book in the New Testament.

Jesus knew that once people developed a *church mentality* or a *Christian mentality,* they would not be effective in administering His kingdom. He knew that a church without a kingdom

> **Jesus never asked us to pray for revival: He asked us to pray for His kingdom to come.**

mindset would be just another mediocre organization that would not bring any change in the community in which it existed. If a local church has lost its influence in its society, then that church has lost its kingdom purpose. That is why He made the comparison to salt that had lost its saltiness. What is it good for?

Jesus never asked us to pray for revival: He asked us to pray for His kingdom to come. I have never seen people crying for His kingdom to come, but I have seen people crying and wailing for revival. No wonder the world is in the shape it is!

I believe His priority to see His kingdom established on the earth can be seen in everything He said and did. Every message was to reveal something of His kingdom and to see one aspect of His kingdom made manifest. Think about it: Jesus' first and last messages were about the kingdom of God (Matthew 4:17; Acts 1:3). The book of Acts also begins and ends with the kingdom message (Acts 1:3; 28:30-31).

"From that time Jesus began to preach and to say, 'Repent, for the kingdom of heaven is at hand' " (Matthew 4:17).

"To whom He [Jesus] also presented Himself alive after His suffering by many infallible proofs, being seen by them during forty days and speaking of the things pertaining to the kingdom of God" (Acts 1:3).

Wherever I go, I see people seeking and hungering for miracles, signs, and wonders. They think that if we produce more miracles the world will come to Jesus. Jesus never asked us to *seek* miracles. There was one group of people in the Bible that were looking

> **Jesus never asked us to *seek* miracles.**

for signs: the religious leaders. They did that because of their unbelief, and Jesus did not commend them for it.

Most people who saw and experienced miracles, both in the Old and New Testaments, did not remain faithful to God. The Israelites saw miracles as well as manifestations of the power of God in Egypt and in the wilderness. They saw more than all other people combined, but the majority of them perished in the wilderness. Did you ever wonder why the crowd that followed Jesus, who ate the bread He multiplied and saw miracles, were not there in the upper room?

Why does the Bible mention miracles and healings? They are "hooks" to catch people to bring them into the kingdom. They are not the end but a means to get people attracted to the kingdom, or Jesus Himself. He told the disciples to go and heal the sick and to tell them that the kingdom of God has arrived (Luke 9:2).

Sadly today we stop at the miracles rather than take people beyond them. We talk about them; we broadcast them; we even shout about them, and then, we end the service. Not very many people go any further. When we seek His kingdom, we find everything we are looking for. Why should we seek just one or two aspects of His kingdom when we can have it all? God has made everything available to His children: everything He has in His kingdom.

What Do You Think about the Kingdom?

What comes to your mind when you hear the word *kingdom* is also important. Many Christians relate *kingdom* with the power of God. Others think of healing or miracles; still others think of helping the poor and those in need. These are all perceptions of the kingdom that have been distorted by the religious spirit.

What comes to your mind when you hear the phrase, "the kingdom of Alexander the Great" or "the kingdom of Persia"? Is it worship, healing, or helping the poor? What comes to your mind when you hear the phrase, "the kingdom of God"?

> If we are supposed to seek the kingdom first and the church is here to administer the kingdom of God, then we need to know what comprises a kingdom.

There has never been a kingdom on this earth that was just made of power or healings. In fact, no kingdom can exist on just power, regardless of what kind of power it is. A kingdom has many components. The most important component of a kingdom is its king. A kingdom is like any other nation except it is ruled by a king. The most important components of a kingdom are the king and the government that administers the king's kingdom.

If we are supposed to seek the kingdom first and the church is here to administer the kingdom of God, then we need to know what comprises a kingdom. A kingdom is made of twelve different components: 1) King, 2) Government/*Ekklesia*, 3) Territory, 4) People, 5) Culture 6) Decrees & Laws, 7) Army,

8) Education/Teachings, 9) Economy/Treasury, 10) Business/ Industry, 11) Media, and 12) Science & Technology.

In the Bible, twelve is the number of divine government. When you hear the term "kingdom of God" I would like you to imagine all twelve ingredients, not just one or two of them, all working together to make a kingdom. There is a reason why there are twelve tribes of Israel and why Jesus selected twelve disciples. As I said earlier, everything God does has a kingdom flavor. The hundred and twenty in the upper room is also twelve multiplied by ten.

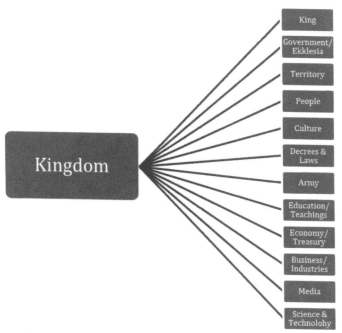

You might wonder why I did not mention miracles, tongues, faith, worship, grace, and other gifts of the Holy Spirit as

> **The gifts of the Holy Spirit are spiritual *tools* or *weapons* to accomplish certain tasks in the kingdom, but they are not the kingdom.**

being part of the kingdom. Some think the kingdom of God is only about power, healing, signs, and miracles. The gifts of the Holy Spirit are spiritual *tools* or *weapons* to accomplish certain tasks in the kingdom, but they are not the kingdom. No nation or kingdom can survive on its military or weapons alone. Others say the kingdom is all about love, righteousness, peace, and joy in the Holy Spirit. That is the *culture* of the kingdom, and again not the whole kingdom.

When we receive the kingdom as a whole and administer it effectively in our communities and nations, then the change we are looking for will happen. If we train our children to do the same, the ground we gain will be retained for generations to come. That is God's heart and that is the mandate of the kingdom of God.

The Kingdom of God and the Kingdom of Heaven

You might ask, "What is the difference between the kingdom of God and the kingdom of heaven?" I remember listening to an argument between some students at the Bible school where I studied. They were having a deep theological debate about those two different terms. I also wondered about it. Why did Jesus use both terms intermittently? One day the Holy Spirit illuminated this to me, "The phrase "kingdom of God" is talking about *who* the kingdom belongs to, like the kingdom of Nebuchadnezzar. The phrase "kingdom of heaven" is referring to *where* it belongs, like the kingdom of Babylon. It was that simple, and I said, "Thank You, Holy Spirit."

The Bible says the kingdom of heaven suffers violence and the violent take it by force (Matthew 11:12). As you know, God lives outside of time. His kingdom is an everlasting kingdom. From God's perspective, He has made available to us everything He has. He did not put any *time limit* on anything; He only put a *faith limit.*

A kingdom or nation is only as good as the *government* that leads it. There are many nations on this earth that are very rich in natural and human resources, but they remain poor for the lack of proper governance. The church is becoming ineffective and irrelevant in many parts of the world. It is not because it has lost its power or authority, but because we don't know how to administer the kingdom God has given us.

> "For he has rescued us out of the darkness and gloom of Satan's kingdom and brought us into the Kingdom of his dear Son" (Colossians 1:13 TLB).

> "Since we have a Kingdom nothing can destroy, let us please God by serving him with thankful hearts and with holy fear and awe" (Hebrews 12:28 TLB).

If the church in any nation or city *used* its power and authority, then not even a little demon would move its pinky to do anything. It would be like Pharaoh told Joseph, "I *am* Pharaoh, and without your consent no man may lift his hand or foot in all the land of Egypt" (Genesis 41:44).

That is the kind of power and authority God wants His church to walk in. Joseph is a *type* of Jesus in the Old Testament. When Pharaoh (God) promoted Joseph in Egypt, he was made to ride on the second chariot and have people cry out before him, saying, "Bow the knee" (Genesis 41:43). You and I know that at the name of Jesus every knee shall bow and every tongue shall confess that He is Lord.

On the other side there are many nations that used to be Christian and had many mighty revivals, but are now losing their Christian heritage. They consider themselves to be living in a post-Christian era. Why is that? Why are nations that were once mightily used by God becoming godless societies? Why are we not able to retain the ground we gained through great revivals after only a few generations?

If we are not careful to learn from our past mistakes, many nations that God is moving in today and where the church is growing quickly will repeat the same pattern after one or two generations. Is there a solution to this problem? I believe there is. The solution is to train people to administer God's kingdom in their communities.

Designed for the Kingdom

It has been God's desire and design for us to dwell in His kingdom from the very beginning. We lost the kingdom because of the fall. We cannot function without a kingdom, good or evil. People were designed by God to live in kingdoms. It is a natural thing for the children of a king to live in their father's kingdom.

Though we sinned and disobeyed our Father, He did not forsake us forever. He had a plan of redemption in place beforehand to get us back into His kingdom. Sinful people cannot dwell in the kingdom of God and function properly.

Sin is an operating system inherent to another kingdom, one that Satan introduced. An acronym for sin is Satanic Information Network. It is always misguided thoughts based on wrong information that produce sin.

> **People were designed by God to live in kingdoms. It is a natural thing for the children of a king to live in their father's kingdom.**

The gospel of the kingdom offers man the "real thing" of all their heart longs for. The purpose, love, joy, peace, significance, provision, and eternal life that come from a relationship with the King of kings and the Lord of lords is found in His kingdom. Jesus is the door to His kingdom. No one can come to the Father except through Him. But, to enter this kingdom, we will go through many tribulations (Acts 14:22).

For a person who is raised on this earth and in the world system, it is not easy to change the way they have been trained to think. We will not learn it in any other way, so God allows us to go through challenges to train us to think differently. That is why when we go through trials and challenges and come out of it, we often say, "Oh, I did not know it worked that way," or, "I did not realize that before," or something similar. That means you just learned something you did not know before and as a result you learned to think differently. That is the purpose of everything we go through after we receive our salvation. God is teaching us how to think differently, and how life works in His kingdom.

Once we are trained to think for ourselves and become mature in the things of God, and understand how He operates, then He does not have to allow us to go through tribulations like we did when we began our walk with Him. Sadly, most people never learn and mature and they die in the wilderness just like the people of Israel, without receiving the fulfillment of their promises. When you understand this, you will be able to count it all joy when you go through various trials and temptations like James tells us (James 1:2-4). They all work for our benefit though we may sometimes feel like we are going to die.

From the moment Jesus began to preach, His passion was for people to rediscover His kingdom, not to take them to heaven. The first thing He preached was, "Repent, for the kingdom of heaven is at hand" (Matthew 4:17). We understood it to mean, "If you repent, I am going to take you to heaven when you die." That is not what He said. He said His kingdom is coming to this earth again; it's very close; and for us to receive and enter into it, we need to repent. *Repent* means to change the way we think. The kingdom way of thinking is opposite to the world's way of thinking.

Jesus brought the kingdom back to us and gave us one more opportunity to enter into His kingdom. "At hand" meant it was about to appear. It was very close. Jesus taught and demonstrated the kingdom to us through His life and ministry. He taught us everything we need to know about the kingdom and its mysteries, everything we need to be able to live in that kingdom instead of Satan's. Jesus' goal was that we would live in it and administer it on the earth.

Jesus came to reveal His kingdom and teach His people how it should operate. He taught about the qualities, culture, principles, mysteries, power, and authority of the kingdom. He came to establish His kingdom here. For a kingdom to function as a kingdom requires certain qualities and characteristics. First of all, a kingdom needs a king, then a territory, people, decrees and laws, an army, a working economy, and so on.

The Kingdom Is Inside of You

The kingdom of God is an invisible kingdom. We cannot see how it operates on the earth with our natural eyes. He put His kingdom inside us and it manifests to the world through the work we do. It is God's desire that His will is done *on this earth as it is in heaven*. This can only be done through human beings because the earth was given to us. The new era of the kingdom of God began to operate with the coming of the Holy Spirit on the day of Pentecost. The *ekklesia* of Jesus' kingdom began to operate from that day. We do not see anyone preaching that the kingdom is at hand after the day of Pentecost.

> **He put His kingdom inside us and it manifests to the world through the work we do.**

The kingdom of God belongs to God and He wants to give it to His children. Jesus said to cheer up, little flock, for it has been the Father's good pleasure to give us the kingdom (Luke 12:32). Only God's children can enter and dwell in His kingdom. God gave the authority to become a child of God to those who believe in Jesus and receive forgiveness of sins. The church's primary purpose is to see God's will accomplished on earth as it is in heaven.

When we come together as the church we are the governing body of the kingdom of God, His *ekklesia*. We need to listen to our King's directions for our region and partner with Him to accomplish that vision. Someone who sees the church should see the kingdom of God. Christ is the Head of the church, the King. We read in 1 Corinthians 14 how a body of believers should function and what should be done when an unbeliever comes in.

> "Therefore if the whole church comes together in one place, and all speak with tongues, and there come in those who are uninformed or unbelievers, will they not say that you are out of your mind? But if all prophesy, and an unbeliever or an uninformed person comes in, he is convinced by all, he is convicted by all. And thus the secrets of his heart are revealed; and so, falling down on his face, he will worship God and report that God is truly among you" (1 Corinthians 14:23-25).

But didn't Jesus say He came to give us life and life more abundantly? Yes, there is no doubt, but sadly, the only thing that is hard to find on this earth today is abundant life. We confuse abundant life with having abundant stuff. There is abundant stuff all around us but people are more miserable than ever before. Jesus was not talking about having abundant stuff, but abundant life, the very life that bubbles out of our inner being regardless of our circumstances or the material things we possess. The Bible says this about Jesus: "In Him was life, and the life was the light of men" (John 1:4). Jesus was the most joyful person that ever lived. How many houses, donkeys, and fishing boats did He own? To my knowledge, none. He did not even have a place of His own to lie down and sleep. But He lived an abundant life. That is something to meditate on.

Most Christians do not live in God's kingdom. They were never taught properly so they live dependent on the world system as their source of joy

> **Most Christians do not live in God's kingdom.**

and satisfaction. If a football team is playing on a Sunday, some Christians will choose football over going to church that day. It's time for the church to prioritize and give the Lord His rightful place in our lives. Either accept Jesus as Lord and serve Him or serve the god of this world. Please don't put one foot in the kingdom in an effort to possess its benefits and keep the other in the world. In the end, it will not work.

Kingdom Mindset

When we think of the church, we should think about it with a kingdom mindset. Before Jesus gave the revelation of the church to Paul, He came to reveal the kingdom of God to His disciples. The first thing they heard from His mouth was about the kingdom of God, not about the church. For three-and-a-half years they were trained and equipped with a kingdom mindset. That's why twelve men were able to reach the entire known world with the gospel of the kingdom in their lifetime.

Again, the most important components of a kingdom are the king and his government. If you go to England and learn the customs of the people there, that will not give you an understanding about the royal family and how they once ruled the world. If you buy one of the rifles the British palace guard uses, that won't make you a royal citizen either. You have to live with them for a long time, read their history, and allow their culture, their beliefs, and their language to permeate your being to have a British mindset. You have to become British. The same is true of every culture.

The reason the church doesn't accomplish much these days is because we don't have a kingdom mindset. How does one kingdom invade another kingdom? In our case, we belong to the kingdom of God and are called to invade the territories that are ruled by the powers of darkness. When a kingdom invades another kingdom, they don't start by defeating the poorest of the poor that are living outside the city walls. They are looking for people in authority who hold key positions.

> **When a kingdom invades another kingdom, they don't start by defeating the poorest of the poor that are living outside the city walls.**

This is why it is important to understand what a kingdom is made of. Whenever God used someone to reach a kingdom He always started at the top and went down from there. That's what kingdoms do. A person with a church mindset will always start at the bottom. When God sent Moses to save His people, He told him to go and speak to the elders of his people and Pharaoh, the king of Egypt, not to the leper colony that was outside the city walls.

When God used Joseph, He started with servants of the king to finally bring Joseph to the king himself. Esther, Mordecai, Nehemiah, and Daniel are more examples. Why did God mention all these in the Bible? He is showing us examples of how to reach a nation so we can learn from them. Unfortunately, instead of learning from these experiences and putting them into practice, most Christians are still waiting for God to do everything.

What do I mean by putting them into practice? The Bible is a book of patterns, examples, types, and principles. Whatever happened to the people of Israel is for our example (1 Corinthians 10:6-11). Instead of waiting for God to send a Joseph, we could train someone to be the Joseph of our day. Joseph did not have universities and law schools accessible to him so God did what He needed to do to prepare him. Today everything we need is at the tip of our fingers, but few are making use of the opportunities we have. People live these days to have fun and with an entitlement mentality. They have become lovers of pleasure rather than lovers of God (2 Timothy 3:1-4).

If someone wants to become a Daniel of our time, he or she has the opportunity to go to college and learn. Other religions like Islam and Mormon have this mindset. They don't come to a country to start orphanages and homes for widows. They come to take over or influence governments and key positions in society where the decisions are made and the mindsets of the people are being shaped. They start schools and buy multinational businesses and media channels that shape the culture and the mindset of the people because they know that if they are going to influence and occupy a society they have to take control of those areas by which a society is made and the people are influenced.

Another denomination that I have seen which has the mindset of the kingdom is the Roman Catholic Church. There are many Catholic nations. From the top government official to the shopkeeper down the road, all are Catholics. They have a good understanding about the natural aspects of the kingdom, which most Charismatics and Pentecostals totally miss.

We are busy arranging crusades or another healing rally and worship night, while these forces are taking over nations left and right. We don't see Muslims holding a crusade, or Mormons arranging an evangelistic meeting. They have a different concept of evangelism. The church needs *kingdom mindset evangelism*. You might have heard of *power evangelism* but not *kingdom evangelism*.

The Mandate of the Kingdom

We have erred in our mission because of a lack of understanding about the mandate King Jesus gave us. If you study the four Gospels in depth there is a divine mystery hidden in each gospel about the kingdom and how it is supposed to accomplish its goal. Only when we understand them, and practice and train our people to do the same, will we see the kingdom of God advancing on the earth.

In each gospel, just before Jesus ascended to heaven He gave a different mandate to His disciples. At first, it was difficult for me to comprehend because they all sounded so diverse and seemed like they were given by different people. I do not know the time frame of each mandate, whether He told them all at the same time or on different occasions, but they are all similar and were given to accomplish one single overarching mandate. They are all different with regard to kingdom perspective, but at the end they accomplish the same ultimate goal.

In Matthew Jesus said to go and make disciples of all nations (Matthew 28:18-19). I call it the *Kingdom Mandate*. How do we disciple a nation? We have miserably failed at discipling the nations because we have been so busy focusing on making converts that we neglected the nations. This is because of our lack of understanding of what makes a nation and how it should be approached.

> **We are busy arranging crusades or another healing rally and worship night, while these forces are taking over nations left and right.**

In the gospel of Mark, Jesus gave a different mandate: To go into all the world and preach the gospel to all creatures and He who believes, signs (casting out demons, speaking in tongues, healing the sick, etc.) will follow (Mark 16:15-18). That is a *Personal Mandate* because it focuses on dealing with people individually, like casting out demons and laying hands on people. We have been practicing that effectively and as a result we have many converts. However, we have not done well in discipling them. We have not discipled the nations well because we are not doing it with a kingdom mindset. We have not discipled converts well either. We have been concerned about taking more people to heaven instead of teaching disciples how to live in God's kingdom on earth.

In Luke, we read about yet another mandate. They are directed to preach repentance and the remission of sins in His name and then told to wait in Jerusalem for the promise of the Father, that they would be endued with power (Luke 24:46-49). This is the *Power Mandate*, which we have been practicing and preaching. As a result we have a great many churches in various nations, but the soul and heart of those nations remain unaffected by the gospel. This is because the church did not understand its real purpose.

In the gospel of John, Jesus did not give a specific mandate like He did in the other three, but demonstrated it. John was the apostle of love. In it we read that God so loved the world that He gave His only begotten Son. His gospel ends with Jesus reconciling Peter to Himself and restoring his faith (John 21:15-18). Love brings reconciliation—it is the very essence of the kingdom. We have been given the ministry of reconciliation (2 Corinthians 5:18). We reconcile people back to God and to each other. I call it the *Love Mandate*. We have not been very effective in executing this mandate either. Unfortunately, we are known more for what we hate than what we love and appreciate.

The time has come for us to pick up where we left off and to redeem the areas where we have not been effective. We need to start with the gospel of Matthew, because that is the first one that preaches the gospel of the kingdom. Every other gospel and their mandates are complementary. They are supposed to work together to accomplish the mandate that was given in Matthew. I strongly believe that the next move of God will be discipling nations by administering His kingdom. We are already in it but as with any new move it takes time for people to change their mindset from the old to the new. This book will help you do that.

When you look at the New Testament and the church, you need to look at them with a kingdom mindset. What comes to your mind when you think of the church? Compare that with what comes to your mind when you think of the kingdom. When you were born again you became a citizen of the kingdom of heaven. A kingdom-minded Christian thinks and functions differently than a church-minded Christian. We will look at the differences in detail in the next chapter.

> **A kingdom-minded Christian thinks and functions differently than a church-minded Christian.**

Chapter 3: The Church Mindset versus the Kingdom Mindset

Chapter 3: The Church Mindset versus the Kingdom Mindset

"And He said to them, 'To you it has been given to
know the mystery of the kingdom of God' "
(Mark 4:11).

In the following pages I would like to explain the difference between how the church as we know it operates and how a kingdom operates, which is the way the church *should* operate. It will help you understand the difference between having a church mindset and a kingdom mindset.

The Kingdom Is Focused on Influence

When we study the book of Acts and the people God reached, we see something significant. God did not reach just anyone. He handpicked people from different nations and languages. He chose people of influence who in turn influenced others and even whole nations. Whenever God does something, He intends to make the maximum impact. He will orchestrate events and circumstances so He can get the most leverage for His glory and the expansion of His kingdom.

God chose the day of Pentecost to send the Holy Spirit. Why would God choose that particular day? With such a large group of people present, He knew He could initiate reaching the entire world at that time with one incident.

Philip the evangelist was led by the Spirit to share the gospel with an Ethiopian eunuch. Why this eunuch? He was the treasurer for the queen of Ethiopia, a man of influence, through whom the entire nation was reached with the gospel.

> **Kings and kingdoms are always reached from the top to the bottom. The church on the other hand starts from the bottom and tries to reach the top, but that doesn't work.**

Kings and kingdoms are always reached from the top to the bottom. The church on the other hand starts from the bottom and tries to reach the top, but that doesn't work. That is why we don't have the influence we should have. It is taking more than two thousand years to do what twelve men accomplished in their lifetime.

The Church Is Focused on Events

Many churches try to keep their people busy with programs and events. One of the intentions of this method is to keep the people attending that particular church, and encourage fellowship and community building.

The Kingdom Wants Effectiveness

In the kingdom, it is not numbers that matter, but effectiveness. Whenever God accomplished something, it was

THE CHURCH MINDSET VERSUS THE KINGDOM MINDSET

not the number that He was concerned with, but the quality and faith of the select few. It's not the size of the church that matters but its effectiveness in administering the kingdom of God in the community and the nation it is in.

The Church Wants Numbers

For some reason we believe that if there are more Christians in a nation, then things will be different. America has more Christians in number, but they don't necessarily have any influence. They aren't forming policy or part of making decisions. History shows that only a handful of people have really affected cultures and history. We don't need another church in America like the majority of the ones we have. We need kingdom-representing churches. We need believers who are thinking and acting like the ambassadors of God's kingdom.

A small number of people have shaped culture and civilization. In his book, *To Change the World,* James Davison Hunter[8] summarizes it this way,

> "Even if we add the minor figures in all of the networks, in all of the civilizations, the total is only 2,700. In sum, between 150 and 3,000 people (a tiny fraction of the roughly 23 billion people living between 600 B.C. and A.D. 1900) framed the major contours of all world civilizations. Clearly, the transformations here were top-down."

8. Hunter, James Davison. *To Change the World: The Irony, Tragedy, and Possibility of Christianity in the Late Modern World.* New York: Oxford University Press, 2010.

The Kingdom Wants to Rule and Establish Dominion

Anytime a kingdom comes into a new region, they are not planning to start orphanages or help the poor. They are thinking about how they can take over the new territory and rule it. The main focus is to establish or take over one of the pillars a kingdom or a nation stands upon, and gain influence. They want to set up an extension of their dominion in that new nation. They may eventually have programs that would help the poor and orphans but that is not their first priority. God is looking for people through whom He can administer His kingdom on this earth now.

The Church Is Waiting to Escape the Earth

There are two topics that excite most Christians today: rapture and revival. Neither of these two words is mentioned in the Bible. Why don't we talk more about what Jesus actually talked about? Why aren't we passionate about what Jesus is passionate about—His kingdom? Jesus did not tell us to focus on His coming. He did not tell us to focus on revivals either.

Jesus was not running around making converts. He did not tell every individual He met, "Hey, if you don't believe in Me and repent, you are going to hell." Instead, He was calm and relaxed. We don't see the apostles doing that either. Jesus was not interested in converts or large crowds. They were actually a distraction to His mission. There were big crowds around Jesus all the time, but they were not all committed to Him or

His cause. In the end, there were only a hundred and twenty people who waited for the promise of the Father.

The Kingdom Is Looking for Citizens

Kingdoms don't look for converts to fill a space in a pew. A convert becomes a liability and does not add any value. They come with a mindset to receive rather than to give. Kingdoms are looking for active citizens who will represent the king, government, and culture wherever they go and through whatever they do.

The Church Wants Converts

On the other hand, the church is looking for converts. At least that's what we have been doing over the past few centuries. Jesus never asked us to go and make converts—He told us to make disciples. We are trying to populate heaven but that is not our mandate. Where did we get that idea? Our mission is not to populate heaven. Our mission is to help the Father and the Son to accomplish their mission on this earth, which is twofold: The Father wants the enemies of His Son brought to His footstool. In turn, the Son will submit all the kingdoms of this earth back to the Father (1 Corinthians 15:24; Revelation 11:15).

The Father gave all authority and power to the Son and the Son gave them to the church, which is you and me. They sent us the Holy Spirit to help us accomplish it. The devil stole the kingdoms of this world from the Father by deceiving us. The question is are we going to honor the Father and the Son for all the love and mercy bestowed upon us?

The Kingdom Operates from a Producer Mentality

Kingdoms are looking to influence. One way to have influence is to have products. God filled this earth with His products. He introduced Himself as the Creator in Genesis 1:1. Because He indwells us it means that the most creative Person in the universe is living within us. The Architect of the planets and galaxies is living in us. We—the church—should be the most creative and productive people on earth.

The Church Operates from a Consumer Mentality

There are two groups of people on this earth: producers and consumers. The producers have influence over the consumers because producers make decisions for the consumers. The church is the largest consuming agency on earth, but we are supposed to be the most productive agency. We have been robbed, lied to, deceived, and kept ineffective till now, but that time is changing.

In most parts of the western world, it is during the so-called Christian holidays that the retailers make most of their money, though they will neither say "Merry Christmas" nor acknowledge the birth of Jesus. How sad it is that gullible Christians throng into those stores to buy stuff they don't need and make the devil richer while they remain poor. In my opinion, we should boycott those stores and not buy anything from them at all. It is time for Christians to stand for what they believe. As the saying goes, "If you don't stand for something, you will fall for anything."

There is a reason for commercializing a holiday. At these times people are prone to spending more money. Even if they don't have the money, many people go into debt to celebrate. Jesus would not have us borrow money to "celebrate His birthday." We give our hard-earned money to the devil and his kingdom to accomplish his agenda while most Christians remain broke. It is totally against God's kingdom principles. His Word says a borrower is a slave to the lender and that we shall not borrow, but lend, to many nations.

The Kingdom Wants to Mentor

One of the reasons the church is not effective today is because there is no effective mentoring on any level. Everyone is trying to be a superhero or a supermodel. If you cannot reproduce yourself or cannot impart to someone what you know, then you really don't know what you think you know. The reason people don't mentor is because they are afraid of losing what they have. If they are busy mentoring, they won't be able to build their own personal kingdoms. The purpose of kingdom mentoring is to restore the image and likeness of God in people, and in turn, to have dominion on the earth.

The Church Wants to Worship

Jesus did not start the church to worship Him. If worship meant singing, I find it interesting that He never asked anyone to sing to Him while He was here. The disciples did not rise early in the morning and sing, "This is the day. This is the day that Jesus made." No. That was not part of their training. The word "worship" appears seventy times in the New Testament in the New King James Version. But, *not even one time does it mean singing*. When I found that out, I said "Wow!"

So much time, effort, and resources are spent today on so-called worship. Its intent is more to entertain or impress people than to please the Lord. The Lord is already pleased with us. We don't need to sing for an hour to please Him or for Him to show up. There have been many services where the presence of the Lord showed up on the first line of the song. They could have started tapping into what the Lord had for them, but they kept on going for another twenty or forty minutes just to make noise and to make the people tired. When it is time to listen to the Word, many are sleepy. Jesus said, "For where two or three are *gathered* together in My name, I am there in the midst of them" (Matthew 18:20).

The Kingdom Is Looking to Give

One of the economic principles of the kingdom is that in order to receive, you first have to give. The good news is you will always have something to give. It may not always be money but you are equipped to bless someone in some way at all times.

The Church Wants to Receive

The church has created a negative impression that we are always trying to get something cheap or for free and then call it favor or a miracle. That's a poverty mindset. The church is supposed to be equipped with all grace so that we always have all sufficiency in all things and have an abundance for every good work (2 Corinthians 9:8).

The Kingdom Produces Kings

God is a king. His children are supposed to be princes and princesses. The first identity we have in the kingdom is that of kings. In relationship with God, we are His children. In His kingdom, we are kings. What does a king do? He takes dominion and reigns.

The Church Produces Christians

The world is going the way it is not because there aren't enough Christians on this planet, but because most Christians do not have a kingdom mindset. Twelve men in the first century reached almost the entire known world with the gospel. We have been trying to do this for more than a century with close to a billion Christians. Christianity is now the name of a religion.

The Kingdom Is Comprised of Sons and Daughters

When you believe in Jesus Christ, God gives you the authority or right to become His child (John 1:12). Most people live in the "believing" stage and never move to the stage of sonship.

Every Sunday and on special holidays, many come and renew their "believing" status, but never grow beyond it. Sons and daughters don't visit a few times a year; they are an integral part of the kingdom.

The Church Is Comprised of Believers

We have many believers, but few true sons and daughters. The whole world is waiting for the manifestation of the sons of God. What would happen to this earth if the entire body of Christ began to act and exercise their authority as children of God here and now?

You, as a son or a daughter of God, are anointed to set free a part of creation from its bondage. That is your purpose. All of creation came under bondage from the fall. We are like sculptors chiseling away part of a rock to set free a beautiful image. That image was always hidden in the rock, but it took the imagination, tools, and the creativity of an artist to bring that image to light. That is the job before each of us.

The Kingdom Has an Eye for Advancement and Taking New Ground

Advancement comes by taking ground. How do we take ground? It's not just by getting people saved. It is through teaching and training those who come to Christ using kingdom principles. Every human being has at least one problem they are struggling with. Through God we have the solutions to those problems.

The Church Is Focused on Outreach

There are many outreach programs, but how effective are they? I have seen outreaches that feed people, but do nothing to help or train them to change their living conditions or mindsets.

That is not kingdom outreach. When a kingdom ministry goes into a neighborhood, they are looking for transformation. They are looking for the ways they can bring the will of God into that area *as it is in heaven*. It will take some serious prayer, planning, strategy, and hard work to train and bring people out of darkness (ignorance) to the light (knowledge) of the gospel. As the old saying goes, if you give a man a fish you will feed him for a day, but if you teach a man to fish you feed him for a lifetime. That is a kingdom mindset.

The Kingdom Is Equipping Its Citizens to Create and Manage Wealth

In Deuteronomy 8:18, God said that it is He who gives power to create wealth to establish His covenant on the earth. The power of God is available for creating wealth. We need to empower people with the proper teaching about how to tap into the power of God to create wealth and use it for kingdom purposes.

The Church Is Looking for Free Money

The church is known for its "free lunch" mentality. Churches are interested in how much money is coming in the offering because that's what sustains a church and keeps it going. It's not the pastor's fault, but it's the way the system works right now.

The Kingdom Is Looking for Ambassadors

The kingdom is looking for ambassadors to send on diplomatic and special assignment missions to preach the gospel of the kingdom. That is what Jesus told His disciples to preach. The King was commissioning His ambassadors to go and represent His kingdom.

The Church Is Looking for Good Preachers

We all like good preachers. We get excited and motivated when we hear a good sermon. Most of the time that excitement and motivation vanishes by five o' clock on Sunday afternoon.

The Kingdom Brings Change through Legislation

If we really want to change cities and nations we need to change the laws and culture. One of the ways this is done is by executing kingdom purposes through strategic prayer.

The Church Likes to Have Gospel Crusades

We have been doing crusades for years. The more money and popularity a ministry has, the more people show up at their crusades. We will gain some converts as a result of crusades, but they will never save a country or a city. Recently, while I was in a particular country, my heart was grieved. I saw churches on every street but there were kids dying of hunger on those same streets. "International" churches were being established and everyone was doing "international" ministry focused on healing and miracles, but no one was caring for the children in the streets. God spoke to me, saying, "A crusade will save souls but it will not save a nation."

The Kingdom Is Looking for Martyrs

The highest honor a citizen has in a kingdom is to give his or her life for the king. Many false religions make false promises to their adherents if they die for their faith. In the kingdom of Jesus, there is a special crown and honor for those who die for their faith.

The Church Is Looking for Goose Bumps

We limit our experience with God and church to having a good emotional feeling. In some circles they call these feelings "goose bumps." If people have goose bumps, they will say it was a great service. It's time to change.

The Citizens of the Kingdom Honor Their King

When a woman came and poured expensive, fragrant oil on Jesus even His disciples became upset, saying, "Why this waste? For this fragrant oil might have been sold for much and given to *the* poor." Jesus said, "For you have the poor with you always, but Me you do not have always" (Matthew 26:8, 11). Through whatever we do, our intention should be to honor God. The Bible says that if we honor Him, He will honor us (1 Samuel 2:30).

The Church Likes to Help the Poor

We have been good at reaching out to the poor. There are many ministries that focus on the poor and feeding the hungry. But how many ministries are there to reach out to the kings/leaders and professionals in our communities?

The Kingdom Wants to Influence Government and Culture

God always starts from the top when He does something or reaches someone: either a nation or family. He always goes to the place and person of influence first.

The Church Is Looking for Reports

Churches like to receive reports of how many people were reached, and how many people were fed, and so on. This is because their focus is on numbers, rather than effectiveness. They are all about quantity instead of quality, and feel that quantity reflects quality, but it does not.

The Next Step

This book is only an *introduction* to the revelation God gave me about the next move of God called the kingdom movement. If you feel a witness in your spirit and want to know more, I encourage you to get the full book, *The Power and Authority of the Church: Equipping the Saints to Administer God's Kingdom on Earth.* If we apply the principles revealed in it, we can win any community or nation to Christ *within ten to fifteen years without a single crusade or healing rally.*

God wants you to be a part of what He is doing on the earth right now. The world has yet to see everything God intended for His church and through His church. The Bible is a book of principles, types, and examples. That means what is mentioned in the Bible is for our example and we have to apply that to our lives. People like Joseph and Daniel were promoted to top levels of leadership in their nations. Unfortunately, the church did not grab that revelation and run with it. We have been waiting for God to raise up more Josephs and Daniels. But He is not going to do that.

How did God use *ONE PERSON* like Joseph, Daniel, Jeremiah, or Esther to bring nations and kingdoms to their knees—something that more than *ONE BILLION* Christians have been trying to do for centuries with little success? Why do the majority of the people on earth remain unreached when twelve men reached almost the whole known world with the gospel of the kingdom in their lifetime? These things happen when the church fails to administer the kingdom of God in the nations. Why does more than half of the population of the world remain unreached, though we have more Christians and churches on the earth today than at any other time in history? This book will answer these and many other questions.

Most importantly, it will help us gain back the ground we have lost as we come to a better understanding of our place in our Father's kingdom and the job He has commissioned each of us to do. May He grant you insight and wisdom to accomplish your purpose. We look forward to hearing from you.

To order a copy of *The Power and Authority of the Church*, please go to www.kingdommandate.net

Or call or write:

Maximum Impact Ministries,
P.O. Box 631460
Littleton, CO 80163-1460

Phone: (720) 420 9873
Email: mim@maximpact.org
www.maximpact.org

More Books by Abraham John

The Three Most Important Decisions of Your Life: Kingdom Secrets to Discover and Fulfill Your Destiny

Keys to Passing Your Spiritual Tests: Unlocking the Secrets to Your Spiritual Promotion

Recognizing God's Timing for Your Life: Discerning God's Timing and Purpose Through Your Daily Circumstances

Overcoming the Spirit of Poverty: How to Know and Fulfill Your Purpose

Seven Kinds of Believers

Also from Maximum Impact Ministries:

Study Guides
7 Dimensions of God's Glory (Free)
7 Dimensions of God's Grace (Free)
7 Kinds of Faith (Free)

To place an order:

Maximum Impact Ministries,
P.O. Box 631460
Littleton, CO 80163-1460

Phone: (720) 420 9873
Email: mim@maximpact.org
www.maximpact.org